BITCOIN

THE BASICS OF BLOCKCHAIN AND
INVESTING IN CRYPTOCURRENCY

By K. Connors

Table of Contents

INTRODUCTION

Bitcoin has been all over the news the last couple of years, but a lot of people are still unaware of what Bitcoin really is. Could Bitcoin be the future of online currency? This is just one of the questions frequently asked about this exciting digital currency.

Bitcoin is a type of electronic currency (Cryptocurrency) that is autonomous from traditional banking and came into circulation in 2009. According to some of the top online traders, Bitcoin is considered the best known digital currency. It relies on computer networks to solve complex mathematical problems in order to verify and record the details of each transaction made.

The Bitcoin exchange rate does not depend on the central bank and there is no single authority that governs the supply of Cryptocurrency. However, the Bitcoin price depends on the level of confidence its users have. The more major companies that accept Bitcoin as a method of payment, the more successful Bitcoin will become.

One of the benefits of Bitcoin is its low inflation risk. Traditional currencies suffer from inflation and they tend to lose their purchasing power each year, as governments continue to use quantitative easing to stimulate the economy.

Bitcoin doesn't suffer from inflation because Bitcoin mining is limited to just 21 million units. That means the release of new Bitcoins is slowing down and the full amount will be mined out within the next couple of decades. Experts have predicted that the last Bitcoin will be mined by 2050.

Bitcoin has a low risk of collapse, unlike traditional currencies that rely on governments. When currencies collapse, it leads to hyperinflation or the wipeout of one's savings in an instant.

The Bitcoin exchange rate is not regulated by any government and is a digital currency available worldwide. Bitcoin is easy to carry; a billion dollars in Bitcoin can be stored on a memory drive and placed in one's pocket. It is much easier to transport compared to paper money.

One disadvantage of Bitcoin is its untraceable nature, as Governments and other organizations cannot trace the source of your funds and as such can attract some unscrupulous individuals.

Unlike other currencies, there are three ways to make money with Bitcoin: saving, trading, and mining. Bitcoin can be traded on open markets, which means you can buy Bitcoin low and sell them high.

More people have accepted the use of Bitcoin and supporters hope that one day, the digital currency will be used by consumers for their online shopping and other electronic deals. Major companies have already begun accepting payments using the virtual currency. Some of the large firms include Fiverr, TigerDirect, and Zynga, among others.

Bitcoin works, but critics have said that the digital currency is not ready to be used by the mainstream because of its volatility. They also point to the hacking of the Bitcoin exchange in the past that has resulted in the loss of several millions of dollars (nothing that hasnn't already happened to any major banking industry). Supporters of digital currencies have said that there are newer exchanges that are supervised by financial experts and venture capitalists. Experts add that there is still hope for the virtual currency system and the predicted growth is huge.

CHAPTER 1

WHAT IS BITCOIN?

Bitcoin is known as the very first decentralized digital currency. They are basically coins that can be sent through the Internet. 2009 was the year Bitcoin was born. The creator's name is unknown; however, the alias Satoshi Nakamoto was given to this person (or persons).

Bitcoin exchange is a new system of money for the internet that works on the concept of digital currency. It initializes the peer to peer payment system for individuals having no central authority; a new concept of cryptocurrency which was initially introduced in 1998. Cryptography controls the creation and transactions of digital money. Bitcoin works through a software system and does not have any central controlling authority so it is equally managed and controlled by its users around the globe.

BITCOIN TRANSACTIONS

Bitcoin transactions are made directly from person to person through the internet. There's no need for a bank or clearinghouse to act as the middle man. Thanks to this, the transaction fees are much lower; they can be used in all the countries around the world. Bitcoin accounts cannot be frozen, prerequisites to open them don't exist, as the same for limits. Every day more merchants are starting to accept them. You can buy anything you want with them.

One can work with the Bitcoin exchange just like it works with any other kind of currency exchange. Just like working with banks, it is easy to make transactions through Bitcoin Exchange. Analogous to physical trade, the user has to pay to purchase Bitcoins. The difference is that the person has to open an account with a Bitcoin Exchanger. The paid asset of the user will be available in the form of digital currency that can be used to purchase any kind of product. Bitcoins can be exchanged with other Bitcoin holders too. This system works similar to the money exchanges in the banks.

Almost in all payment systems, the payments can be reversed after making a transaction through PayPal or credit cards. But with Bitcoin, the situation is changed, as after making a transaction, one cannot get it back or reverse it. So be careful while exchanging your Bitcoins with currency mediums because you may face chargeback issues. It is preferable to make exchanges with other Bitcoin holders near to you.

It's possible to exchange dollars, Euros or other currencies into Bitcoin. You can buy and sell as it were any other country's currency. In order to keep your Bitcoins, you have to store them in something called wallets. These wallets are located on your pc, mobile device or on third party websites. Sending Bitcoins is very simple. It's as simple as sending an email. You can purchase practically anything with Bitcoins.

When doing a Bitcoin transaction, there's no need to provide the real name of the person. Each one of the Bitcoin transactions recorded is what is known as a public log. This log contains only wallet IDs and not people's names. So basically each transaction is private. People can buy and sell things without being tracked.

WHY BITCOINS?

Bitcoin can be used anonymously to buy any kind of merchandise. International payments are extremely easy and very cheap. The reason for this is that Bitcoins are not really tied to any country. They're not subject to any kind of regulation. Small businesses love them because there are no credit card fees involved. There are also individuals who buy Bitcoins just for the purpose of investment, expecting them to raise their value.

WAYS OF ACQUIRING BITCOINS

1.   Buy on an exchange: People are allowed to buy or sell Bitcoins from sites called Bitcoin exchanges. They do this by using their country currencies or any other currency they have or like.

2.   Transfers: Persons can easily send Bitcoins to each other by their mobile phones, computers or by online platforms. It's the same as sending cash in a digital form.

3.   Mining: The network is secured by people called miners. They're rewarded regularly for all newly verified transactions.

These transactions are fully verified and then they are recorded in what's known as a public transparent ledger. These individuals compete to mine these Bitcoins, by using computer hardware to solve difficult math problems. Miners invest a lot of money in hardware. Nowadays, there's something called cloud mining. By using cloud mining, miners just invest money in third party websites; these sites provide the entire required infrastructure, reducing hardware and energy consumption expenses.

WHERE DO YOU STORE BITCOIN?

These Bitcoins are stored in what is called digital wallets. These wallets exist in the cloud or on people's computers. A wallet is something similar to a virtual bank account. These wallets allow persons to send or receive Bitcoins, pay for things or just save the Bitcoins. As opposed to bank accounts, these Bitcoin wallets are never insured by the FDIC.

TYPES OF WALLETS

1.   Wallet in the cloud: The advantage of having a wallet in the cloud is that people don't need to install any software on their computers and wait for long syncing processes. The disadvantage is that the cloud may be hacked and people may lose their Bitcoins. Nevertheless, these sites are very secure.

2.   Wallet on the computer: The advantage of having a wallet on the computer is that people keep

their Bitcoins secured from the rest of the internet. The disadvantage is that people may delete them by formatting the computer or because of viruses.

HOW TO SETUP A BITCOIN ACCOUNT

You can acquire a Bitcoin wallet from a Bitcoin broker such as Blockchain. When you open up a wallet through a certified broker, you are given a Bitcoin address which is a series of numbers and letters, similar to an account number for a bank account and a private key which is a series of numbers and letters as well, which serves as your password.

HOW DO YOU SEND BITCOIN?

In order to pay for goods and services or to send Bitcoins to an individual, 3 things are needed. Your Bitcoin address, your private key, and the recipient's Bitcoin address. From that point, through your Bitcoin wallet, you will send three pieces of information, which are: input, balance, and output. Input refers to your address, balance refers to a number of Bitcoins you are going to send and output is the recipient's address.

BENEFITS OF BITCOIN EXCHANGE

1.   No taxation

When you make purchases via dollars, Euros or any other government fiat currency, you have to pay an additional sum of money to the government as tax. Every purchasable item has its own designated tax rate. However, when you're making a purchase through Bitcoin, sales taxes are not added to your purchase. This is deemed as a legal form of tax evasion and is one of the major advantages of being a Bitcoin user.

With zero tax rates, Bitcoin can come in handy especially when purchasing luxury items that are exclusive to a foreign land. Such items, more often than not, are heavily taxed by the government.

2.   Flexible online payments

Bitcoin is an online payment system and just like any other such system, the users of Bitcoin have the luxury of paying for their coins from any corner of the world that has an internet connection. This means that you could be lying on your bed and purchasing coins instead of taking the pain of traveling to a specific bank or store to get your work done.

Moreover, an online payment via Bitcoin does not require you to fill in details about your personal information. Hence, Bitcoin transactions are a lot simpler than those carried out through U.S. Bank accounts and credit cards.

3.   Minimal transaction fees

Fees and exchange costs are a part and parcel of standard wire transfers and international purchases. Bitcoin is not monitored or moderated by any intermediary institution or government agency. Therefore, the costs of transacting are kept very low unlike international transactions made via conventional currencies.

In addition to this, transactions in Bitcoin are not known to be time-consuming since it does not involve the complications of typical authorization requirements and waiting periods.

4.   Concealed user identity

All Bitcoin transactions are discrete, or in other words, Bitcoin gives you the option of user anonymity. Bitcoins are similar to cash only purchases in the sense that your transactions can never be tracked back to you and these purchases are never connected with your personal identity. As a matter of fact, the Bitcoin address that is created for user purchases is never the same for two different transactions. If you want to, you do have the option of voluntarily revealing and publishing your Bitcoin transactions, but in most cases, users keep their identities private.

5.   No outside interventions

One of the greatest advantages of Bitcoin is that it eliminates third party interruptions. This means that governments, banks, and other financial intermediaries have no authority whatsoever to disrupt user transactions or freeze a Bitcoin account. As mentioned before, Bitcoin is based strictly on a peer to peer system. Hence, the users of Bitcoin enjoy greater liberty when making purchases with Bitcoins than they do when using conventional national currencies.

WHAT OTHER CRYPTOCURRENCIES EXIST?

This is a list of cryptocurrencies. There were more than 900 cryptocurrencies available over the internet as of the time of writing this book and growing. By market capitalization, Bitcoin is currently the largest blockchain network, followed by Ethereum, Bitcoin Cash, Ripple, and Litecoin.

CURRENCY - RELEASE DATE

Bitcoin - 2009

Litecoin - 2011

Namecoin - 2011

SwiftCoin - 2011

PeerCoin - 2012

DogeCoin - 2013

EmerCoin - 2013

GridCoin - 2013

PrimeCoin - 2013

Ripple - 2013

AuroraCoin - 2014

BlackCoin - 2014

BurstCoin - 2014

Coinye - 2014

Dash - 2014

DigitalNote - 2014

MazaCoin - 2014

Monero - 2014

NEM - 2014

Nxt - 2014

PotCoin - 2014

Synereo AMP - 2014

TitCoin - 2014

VertCoin - 2014

Ethereum - 2015

IOTA - 2015

SixEleven - 2015

Zcash - 2016

Bitcoin Cash - 2017

BitConnect - 2017

WHAT TO LOOK FOR IN CRYPTOCURRENCIES

Cryptocurrencies use a number of different algorithms and are traded in different ways. Here are the main characteristics that you should consider.

1.   Market capitalization and daily trading volume

A cryptocurrency's market capitalization is the total worth of all coins currently in circulation. A high market capitalization can indicate a high value per coin or simply a lot of available coins. Perhaps more important than market capitalization is daily trading volume: the value of the coins that exchange hands every day. A high daily trading volume relative to the market capitalization indicates a healthy economy with many transactions.

2.   Verification method

One of the major differences between cryptocurrencies is their verification method. The oldest and most common method is called proof of work. To gain the right to verify a transaction, a computer has to expend time and energy solving a difficult math problem. The trouble with this method is that it requires a massive amount of energy to operate. Proof-of-stake systems attempt to solve this problem by letting the users with the largest share of the currency verify the transactions.

These systems require less processing power to operate and claim faster transaction speeds, but concern over security means that few coins use an entirely proof-of-stake-based system.

3.   Retailer acceptance

A cryptocurrency isn't much use if you can't buy anything with it. That's why it's important to know who accepts a currency before you invest in it. A few cryptocurrencies are widely accepted, even boasting partnerships with major retailers. Most, however, have more limited acceptance, and some can only be exchanged for other cryptocurrencies. Some coins simply aren't designed to be exchanged for goods and are built for other purposes.

Cryptocurrencies are an exciting new development in the world of finance. No one is quite sure yet where the technology will lead, but the fact remains that these new currencies offer possibilities that traditional cash can't.

CHAPTER 2

WHAT IS BLOCKCHAIN?

Blockchain is an irrefutably resourceful invention which is bringing about a revolution in the global business market. Its evolution has brought with it a greater good, not only for businesses but for its beneficiaries as well. But since its revelation to the world, a vision of its operational activities is still unclear. The main question that sticks in everyone's mind is - What is Blockchain?

To start with, Blockchain technology serves as a platform that allows the transit of digital information without the risk of being copied. It has, in a way, laid the foundation of a strong backbone of a new kind of internet space. Originally designed to deal with Bitcoin - trying to explain to the layman about the functions of its algorithms, the hash functions, and digital signature property, today, technology buffs are finding other potential uses of this immaculate invention which could pave the way to the onset of an entirely new business dealing process in the world.

Blockchain, to define in all respects, is a kind of algorithm and data distribution structure for the management of electronic cash without the intervention of any centralized administration, programmed to record all the financial transactions as well as everything that holds value.

THE WORKING OF BLOCKCHAIN

Blockchain can be comprehended as Distributed Ledger technology which was originally devised to support the Bitcoin cryptocurrency. But post heavy criticism and rejection, the technology was revised for use in more productive things.

To give a clear picture, imagine a spreadsheet that's practically augmented across a plethora of computing systems. And then imagine that these networks are designed to update this spreadsheet from time to time. This is exactly what blockchain is.

Information that's stored on a blockchain is a shared sheet whose data is reconciled from time to time. It's a practical way that speaks of many obvious benefits. To being with, the blockchain data doesn't exist in one single place.

This means that everything stored in there is open for public view and verification. Further, there isn't any centralized information storing platform which hackers can corrupt. It's practically accessed over a million computing systems side-by-side, and its data can be consulted by any individual with an internet connection.

Blockchain technology is something that mimics the internet space. It's robust in nature. Similar to offering data to the general public through the World Wide Web, blocks of authentic information are stored on blockchain platforms which are identically visible on all networks.

Vital to note, blockchain cannot be controlled by a single person, entity or identity, and has no one point of failure. Just like the internet has proven itself as a durable space for the last 30 years, blockchain too will serve as an authentic, reliable global stage for the business transaction as it continues to develop.

USERS OF BLOCKCHAIN

There isn't a defined rule or regulation about who shall or can make use of this technology. Though at present, its potential users are banks, commercial giants and global economies only. The technology is open for the day to day transactions of the general public as well. The only drawback blockchain is facing is global acceptance.

CHAPTER 3

HOW TO BUY AND SELL BITCOIN

HOW TO BUY BITCOIN

Here are some simple steps to buy Bitcoin

1.   Find a wallet

First of all, you have to find an e-wallet. It is basically a store or a provider that offers software from where Bitcoins can be bought, stored, and traded. You can easily run it on your desktop, laptop, and even smartphones.

2.   Sign up

Next, you have to sign up with e-wallet. You will make an account that will let you store your Bitcoins. The e-wallet trader will offer you a chance to convert your local currency into Bitcoin. Therefore, the more local currency you have, the more Bitcoins you can purchase.

3.   Connect your bank account

After signing up, the trader has to connect his or her bank account with their trading account. For this purpose, some verification steps are to be performed. Once the verifications are performed, then you can start purchasing Bitcoins and get started.

4.   Buying and selling

Once you are done with your first purchase, your bank account will be debited and you will receive the Bitcoins. Selling is done in the same way purchasing is done. Keep in mind that the price of Bitcoin changes from time to time. The e-wallet you are working with will show you the current exchange rate. You should be aware of the rate before you buy or sell.

5.   Mining Bitcoin

There is another way through which you can purchase Bitcoins. This process is known as mining. The mining of Bitcoins is similar to discovering gold from a mine. However, as mining gold is time-consuming and a lot of effort is required, the same is the case with mining Bitcoins.

You have to solve a series of mathematical calculations that are designed by computer algorithms to win Bitcoin.. This is nearly impossible for a newbie. Traders have to open a series of padlocks in order to solve the mathematical calculations. In this procedure, you do not have to involve any kind of money to win Bitcoins, as it is simply brainwork that lets you win Bitcoins for free. The expensive part comes when you start using technology to solve these math problems for you. The miners then have to run software in order to win additional Bitcoins.

HOW TO SELL BITCOIN

Selling Bitcoin isn't quite as straight forward as buying Bitcoin, but fortunately, I'm here to help. When deciding how to sell your Bitcoin, you first need to consider which method best suits your situation: selling Bitcoin online or selling Bitcoin in person. Each option has its own advantages and disadvantages.

1.   Selling Bitcoin online

Selling Bitcoin online is by far the more common way of trading. There are now three ways to go about selling Bitcoin online.

a)   The first way involves a direct trade with another person, an intermediary facilitating the connection.

b)   The second way is through an online exchange, where your trade is with the exchange rather than another individual.

c)   New peer-to-peer trading marketplaces that allow Bitcoin owners to obtain discounted goods with their Bitcoin via others that want to obtain the cryptocurrency with credit/debit cards. The two groups are brought together to solve both problems in a kind of peer-to-peer exchange.

SELLING BITCOIN IN PERSON

Selling Bitcoin in person can, in many ways, be the easiest way to pass on your digital currency. Simply scanning a QR code on another person's phone and accepting cash-in-hand is about as easy as a Bitcoin transaction can get.

If you have friends or family who want to buy Bitcoin, the process is simple. Set them up with a

Bitcoin wallet, send them the Bitcoins and collect your cash.

There are several things to be aware of when selling Bitcoin in person.

Agree on a price: Decide on a rate that works for you: Many use a price from a prominent Bitcoin exchange. Some sellers apply a percentage on top of these rates to cover costs and as a convenience/anonymity premium.

You could use a mobile app to calculate prices. It helps to be aware of local fluctuations in price. Price can vary from country to country, often due to difficulties in obtaining Bitcoin with the local national currency. There are many Bitcoin meetups around the world where people are happy to trade Bitcoin and other cryptocurrencies.

Bitcoin is a digital currency that is here to stay for a long time. Ever since it has been introduced, the trading (buying and selling) of Bitcoin has increased and it is on the rise even today. The value of Bitcoin has also increased with its popularity. It is a new type of currency, which many traders are finding attractive just because of its earning potential. At some places, Bitcoins are even being used for purchasing commodities. Many online retailers are accepting Bitcoin for the real time purchases too. There is a lot of scope for Bitcoin in the coming era, and investors seem to be flocking at every chance they can get to purchase a coin here and there.

CHAPTER 4

INVESTING STRATEGIES FOR BITCOIN

This digital rush of money that is sweeping the global investors is not only getting easier, but also riskier everyday. While it was initially a simple peer-to-peer system for small transactions, it is now used for major investments and foreign luxury purchases, which has introduced newer strategies and uses. How does it really work?

Bitcoin is a currency just like any other. It can not only be used to buy and sell, but can be used for investing and sharing, and can even be stolen. While the initial introduction of the technology came with a desktop program, it can now be directly operated through a Smartphone application, which allows you to immediately buy, sell, trade or even cash your Bitcoins for dollars.

Investment with Bitcoins has become very popular, with major sums of money being put in everyday. As a new investor, the rules remain the same as investing with real cash. Do not invest more than you can afford to lose, and do not invest without a goal. Or, as Warren Buffet would say, "Never invest in something you know nothing about". For every trade, keep certain milestones in mind. The 'buy low and sell high' strategy is not as easy implemented as said. A great way to succeed faster when you decide to trade Bitcoins, however, is to learn the technicalities. Like cash investments, there are now several Bitcoin charting tools to record the marketing trends and make predictions to help you make investment decisions. Even as a beginner, learning how to use charting tools and how to read charts can go a long way. A normal chart will usually include the opening price, the closing price, the highest price, the lowest price and the trading range, which are the essentials you need before making any sale or purchase. Other components will give you different information about the market.

Moreover, new investors will often quickly open unprofitable positions. With this, however, remember that you have to pay an interest rate for every 24 hours that the position is kept open, with the exception of the first 24 hours that are free. Therefore, unless you have a sufficient balance to cover the high-interest rate, do not keep any unprofitable position open for more than 24 hours.

While Bitcoin trading still has its drawbacks, like transactions taking too long to complete and no reversing option, it can benefit you greatly with investing, provided that you take small steps in the right direction.

Note: A good investment strategy -

If you are interested in Bitcoin as an investment, you might consider following my simple investment strategy:

a)   Buy Bitcoins, and keep them for a relatively long period of time. Resist the temptation to buy more or sell unless you've thought about it very carefully. Just like buy and hold property investing, the long game wins more often than the short game.

b)   If you are a technical expert, you might want to make bets on emerging cryptocurrencies, but only for a short time and only at the beginning. This behavior is more speculation than wise investing. Do it at your own risk.

c)   Do not day trade: Unless you are a professional trader, do not day trade with Bitcoin. Commissions are high, you are probably influenced by something you've just read, and you are defenseless against market manipulation and pump and dump schemes which are still very common.

d)   Have a plan: Bitcoin investors need to have a strategy: It could be trying to pay off student loans, trying to retire, etc. These different strategies will provide a framework to make a risk reward tradeoff decision.

CHAPTER 5

HOW TO MINE BITCOIN

Before you start mining Bitcoin, it's useful to understand what Bitcoin mining really means. Bitcoin mining is legal and is accomplished by running SHA256 double round hash verification processes in order to validate Bitcoin transactions and provide the requisite security for the public ledger of the Bitcoin network. The speed at which you mine Bitcoins is measured in hashes per second.

The Bitcoin network compensates Bitcoin miners for their effort by releasing Bitcoin to those who contribute the needed computational power. This comes in the form of both newly issued Bitcoins and from the transaction fees included in the transactions validated when mining Bitcoins. The more computing power you contribute, the greater your share of the reward.

Of course, there's only one place Bitcoins really come from: MINING. Every Bitcoin you'll ever own, see, or hear about, was at one point mined via the

Bitcoin mining network. If you find yourself in possession of a mining rig, go ahead and mine away! Or if you have a computer fast enough to make it worthwhile, that works too.

But be careful! If your computer isn't cooled properly, you run the risk of overheating it, which could potentially break it. Frankly, mining with your computer isn't really worth it. Not anymore. As the mining difficulty increases, it becomes more and more difficult to gain any profit from it. Unless you have a dedicated mining rig, your chance of getting any sort of return from mining is really pretty low.

For Bitcoins, there's an alternative way to hold the necessary records of the transaction history of the entire circulation, and all this is managed via a decentralized manner. The ledger that facilitates the process is known as the "blockchain". The essence of this ledger might require tons of newsprint for appearing regularly at all popular Bitcoin news. Blockchain expands every minute, existing on the machines involved in the huge Bitcoin network. People may question the validity, even authenticity, of these transactions and their recordings into Blockchain.

This too is justified, through the process of Bitcoin mining. Mining enables the creation of new Bitcoin and compiling transactions to the ledger. Mining essentially entails the solving of complex mathematical calculations, and the miners employ immense computing power to solve it. The individual or 'pool' that solves the puzzle, place the subsequent block and wins a reward too. And, how can mining avoid double-spending? Almost every 10 minutes, outstanding transactions are mined into a block. So, any inconsistency or illegitimacy is completely ruled out.

For Bitcoins, mining is not spoken of in a traditional sense of the term. Bitcoins are mined by utilizing cryptography. A hash function termed as "double SHA-256" is employed. But how difficult is it to mine Bitcoins? This can be another query. This depends a lot on the effort and computing power being employed into mining. Another factor worth mentioning is the software protocol. For every block, difficulty entailed in the mining of Bitcoins is adjusted by itself simply to maintain the protocol. In turn, the pace of block generation is kept consistent. A Bitcoin difficulty chart is a perfect measure to demonstrate the mining difficulty over time. The difficulty level adjusts itself to go up or down in a directly proportional manner, depending on the computational power, whether it's being fuelled or taken off. As the number of miner's rise, the percentage of profits deserved by the participants diminishes, everyone ends up with smaller slices of the profits.

MINING BITCOINS

In simple terms, we can define Bitcoin mining as the process of adding transactions to your ledger. The process aids in confirming that enough computational effort is devoted to a block. The process also creates new Bitcoins in each block.

To mine, you should take a look at the transactions in a block and then verify their validity. You should then select the most recent transactions in the header of the most recent block and insert them into the new block as a hash. Before a new block is added to the local blockchain, you have to solve the proof of work problem. This is a problem that is designed to ensure that the new block to be created is difficult and the data used in making the block satisfies the laid down requirements.

Bitcoin uses the Hash cash proof of work; therefore, for you to solve the problem you need to create a hash.

HOW TO CREATE A HASH

If you know how to do it, it's very easy to produce a hash from a collection of Bitcoin blocks. The unfortunate thing is that you can't work out the data by simply looking at the hash - you need to test different blocks.

Hashes are found at the blocks and you have to combine them to prove that your data is legitimate. There are some miners who try to take the easy route by trying to fake a transaction by changing an already stored block.

You should note that each hash is unique and specific to a given block; therefore, when you manipulate a given block, you change the hash. When a given miner runs a hash tag function on the manipulated block, the block is found to be fake, and you won't get any rewards.

MINING REWARD

When you successfully solve a proof of work, you get a mining reward. The number of Bitcoins in the reward depends on a number of factors such as complexity of the problem. For you to make more money you have to solve many problems. You also need to have high-speed computers to enable you to solve as many problems as possible.

Currently, mining pools have sprung up and are founded on a very simple concept. Here a group of miners come together and work on a number of blocks. Once the problem is solved, the miners share the rewards.

HOW TO START BITCOIN MINING

To begin mining Bitcoins, you'll need to acquire Bitcoin mining hardware. In the early days of Bitcoin, it was possible to mine with your computer CPU or high-speed video processor card. Today that's no longer possible. Custom Bitcoin ASIC chips offer performance up to 100x the capability of older systems and have come to dominate the Bitcoin mining industry.

Bitcoin mining with anything less will consume more in electricity than you are likely to earn. It's essential to mine Bitcoins with the best Bitcoin mining hardware built specifically for that purpose.

Many companies started making chips that are exclusively used for running the cryptographic algorithms of this process. Antminer is a popular ASIC hardware used for drawing out Bitcoin. Antminer comes with different specifications such as U1 and U2+. Both U1 and U2+ are about the same size. While U1 has a default hash rate of 1.6 GH/s, U2+ has the hash rate of 2.0 GH/s. The process of entering the Bitcoins transactions in the public ledger is known as, wait for it.. Bitcoin mining. They are introduced into the system through this process. The Bitcoin miner can earn transaction fees and subsidy for the newly created coins. ASIC (Application Specific Integrated Circuit) is a microchip specifically designed for this process. When compared to previous technologies, they are faster. The service offered by the Bitcoin miner is based on specified performance. They provide a specific level of production capacity for a set price.

With the right information and tools, Bitcoin mining is not only rewarding, it's also a fun and safe way to transfer money across the internet. To make as much money as possible you need to have the right software and powerful computer hardware.

BITCOIN CLOUD MINING

If you want to invest in Bitcoin mining without the hassle of managing your own hardware, there is an alternative. You can use the cloud to earn your coins. Put very simply, cloud mining means using (generally) shared processing power run from remote data centers. One only needs a home computer for communications, optional local Bitcoin wallets and so on.

However, there are certain risks associated with cloud mining that investors need to understand prior to purchasing.

PROS

Here's why you might want to consider cloud mining:

- A quiet, cooler home – no constantly humming fans
- No added electricity costs
- No equipment to sell when mining ceases to be profitable

- No ventilation problems with hot equipment
- Reduced chance of being let down by mining equipment suppliers.

CONS

Here's why you might not want to consider cloud mining:

- Risk of fraud
- Opaque mining operations
- Lower profits – the operators have to cover their costs after all
- Contractual warnings that mining operations may cease depending on the price of Bitcoin
- Lack of control and flexibility.

TYPES OF CLOUD MINING

In general, there are three forms of remote mining available at the moment:

1.   Hosted mining

Lease a mining machine that is hosted by the provider.

2.   Virtually hosted mining

Create a (general purpose) virtual private server and install your own mining software.

3.   Leased hashing power

Lease an amount of hashing power, without having a dedicated physical or virtual computer. (This is, by far, the most popular method of cloud mining.)

CHAPTER 6

HOW BITCOIN HAS THE ABILITY TO TAKE OVER AS THE WORLDS CURRENCY

With recent research suggesting that the number of active Bitcoin users is set to approach five million by 2019, the issue of whether the cryptocurrency has the potential to become a global currency is being hotly debated in both the technology and financial worlds.

The key to this currency is that it enables quick and cheap online payments without the need for traditional banking channels. One of the biggest barriers that it has to overcome is the general acceptance of Bitcoin being safe and stable as there is no government regulating it, unlike most currencies. Instead, Bitcoin self-regulates and new coins are issued at the pace at which the miners produce the coins. This is a positive, though, as it is designed to be difficult to create coins so that there is a steady stream of coins being produced.

Bitcoins have been successful in becoming more mainstream with companies such as Microsoft, Dell and Tesla adopting the currency. But transactions are not just limited to bigger companies, with much smaller companies also following suit: you can now order flowers, pizza or coffee with Bitcoins.

As the growth in the adoption of the currency with retailers expands and awareness of the currency increases, so should the confidence in Bitcoin. But there is a large obstacle stopping the currency from becoming mainstream, which is being included in the exchanges. In March 2017, the first proposal for a Bitcoin Exchange Trading Fund was rejected by US regulators, in what could have been a real game changer for Bitcoin but instead saw their currency price fall. With the failure to be accepted by the large institutions, it makes it difficult to see how Bitcoin can grow and become a widely accepted and adopted currency. Further attempts are being made to get Bitcoin listed, which will likely determine its success.

BITCOIN AS A VEHICLE FOR INTERNATIONAL TRAVEL

The phenomenon of Bitcoins has taken over the financial and business world by storm. In a world where convenience is put at a premium, most people want to deal with something handy and avoid too much hassle. Being a virtual currency, Bitcoins have gradually started replacing the bulky traditional bank notes and cheques. Businesses and banks are conducting awareness campaigns for their customers to take up this mode of payment, as it is stress-free and time-saving. The main advantage is that you can track past transactions and exchange rates on a Bitcoin Chart. The following are further reasons why you should put Bitcoins on your list of must-haves:

1.   Universal

When you are traveling, the process of exchanging currency is quite cumbersome. This is worse when you are going to more than one destination. In addition, carrying large amounts of cash is not only tiresome but also risky. Bitcoins give you the comfort of carrying as much money as you need in a virtual state. It is common among traders all over the world and hence saves you the inconvenience of dealing with more than one currency.

2.   Less costly

When you trade using cash, you are subject to abrupt price changes in essential commodities. You end up spending much more than you had budgeted because of punitive exchange rates. Bitcoins are a global currency that has stable rates and value and will save you the time and high fees.

3.   Secure

Bitcoins are fraud proof due to the heavy cryptography that goes into its making. There are no incidences of hacking or leaking of people's personal information. When you use the conventional money transfer methods abroad, you are likely to fall into the hands of hackers who might infiltrate your bank accounts. With Bitcoin, you alone have access to your account and can authorize any money into and from it.

4.   Irreversible

As a seller, you have probably experienced a situation where a client reverses an already complete transaction. Bitcoin protects you from such incidences, as these transfers cannot be reversed. You should be careful with your Bitcoins, however, as to avoid transferring them to the wrong person.

5.   Convenient

Unlike normal banks that require proof of identification to open an account, Bitcoins allow anyone to access it without asking for proof. Transactions are instant and are not limited by geographical boundaries or time zones, and there is no paperwork involved. To trade Bitcoins, you only need to download the Bitcoin wallet and create an account. You will also never be turned away from opening a Bitcoin account if you are on Chex Systems or owe money to a financial institution.

CHAPTER 7

HOW BUSINESSES CAN BEGIN ACCEPTING BITCOIN

Bitcoins are taking over the crypto-currency marketplace. They're the largest and most well-known digital currency. Many large companies are accepting Bitcoins as a legitimate source of funds, meaning they allow their online products to be bought with Bitcoins. With the extreme facilitation of transfer and earning of Bitcoins, it would be a mistake not to accept these new-found online coins as cash.

HOW CAN BUSINESSES BEGIN ACCEPTING BITCOIN?

1.   Creating your Bitcoin address

First, you will need a Bitcoin wallet. This is the address where customers will send their money, and that process works a lot like email: they input your address (or, more likely, scan your QR code with their smartphones), enter the desired amount and hit "Send."

Like with a cash register, you will probably need to take the money out at the end of the business day and store it somewhere safe. In general, it is good practice to keep only small amounts of Bitcoins on your computer, mobile, or server for everyday use. You may want to store the bulk of your funds in a safer environment. Make sure you use some best practices for securing your business wallet.

2.   Using a payment processor

When introducing Bitcoin to your business, find the best suitable payment processor or the best Bitcoin merchant solution that enables accepting Bitcoins. To make things easy and to protect yourself against the high volatility that affects Bitcoin, find a partner that can manage the process by allowing you to accept Bitcoin payments but instantaneously converting it into FIAT currency. This way, you will be getting your payment in national currency without even having to deal directly with Bitcoin.

Below, you will find a list of some of the most well-known Payment Processors:

- BitKassa – Merchant accepting Bitcoin solution,
- BitPagos – Bitcoin and Credit Card payment processor

- BitPay – Bitcoin payment processor with mobile checkout solution
- Bitbay – Bitcoin payment processor with mobile checkout solution
- BitPOS – Bitcoin payment processor for online and brick and mortar stores
- Coinbase – Offers payment buttons, checkout pages, shopping cart integration, and daily cash out to USD.
- Coinify – Bitcoin Web Payments, Mobile Checkout, In-store Bitcoin Payments and Bitcoin Invoicing with recurring billing in Bitcoin.
- Coinkite – Full-reserve banking, payment buttons, invoice pages, hardware POS terminals, and Debit-Cards.
- GoCoin – International payment gateway and processing platform for Merchants
- XBTerminal – Brick-and-mortar hardware POS terminals with payment processing integrations.

Payment processors will charge either a percentage or a monthly fee for their services, but their prices are still far cheaper than what credit card companies or PayPal charge.

Furthermore, payment processors will offer a few applications of their technology: you can send email invoices, set up a POS (useful if you are running a restaurant or cafe, for example) or add a shopping cart plug-in to your online shop.

Finally, if you don't want to hold onto your Bitcoin (say your suppliers and landlord want cash in fiat), these kinds of processors can convert your money into fiat instantly.

3.   Advertise Bitcoin acceptance

It helps a lot to indicate to your customers that you do, in fact, accept Bitcoin. If you have an online storefront, grab a "Bitcoin Accepted Here" banner and paste it on your site, ideally beside your PayPal, MasterCard, Visa and whatever buttons you already have.

If you have a brick-and-mortar establishment, grab similar stickers for your door or cash register here.

4.   Bookkeeping and Taxes

Reach out to your accountant to determine how to keep records of Bitcoin transactions. Some accountancy firms are beginning to emerge that specialize in Bitcoin and other cryptocurrencies.

WHY SHOULD YOU START ACCEPTING BITCOIN?

The main reasons that drive businesses to integrate Bitcoin as a payment method:

1. Lower Transaction fees: Bitcoin can reduce credit card processing fees to less than 1%.

2. No Chargebacks: Bitcoin transactions are irreversible, so it automatically prevents having chargeback's or returns, like what happens with credit cards.

3. Facilitates International Transfers: Small online retailers and other businesses avoid selling their wares and services internationally because of expensive cross-border transaction fees. Bitcoin relieves the steep cost of international transactions by enabling easier, faster and cheaper cross-border payments.

4. Fraud Prevention: Bitcoin provides a level of identity-theft protection that credit cards and other banking services are simply not able to offer. Once you receive payment, it will never be disputed.

5. Faster Payments with less cost: Having funds immediately available is critical for the survival of many small businesses. By accepting Bitcoin payments, you have access to funds immediately, which is available much faster than with credit card payments.

LIST OF COMPANIES WHO ACCEPT BITCOINS AS PAYMENT

Many companies are accepting Bitcoins, many are not. Here is a list of the biggest names who accept Bitcoins as a currency.

- WordPress.com – An online company that allows user to create free blogs
- Overstock.com – A company that sells big ticket items at lower prices due to overstocking
- Subway – Eat Fresh
- Microsoft – Users can buy content with Bitcoin on Xbox and Windows Store
- Reddit – You can buy premium features there with Bitcoins
- Virgin Galactic – Richard Branson Company that includes Virgin Mobile and Virgin Airline
- OkCupid – Online dating site
- Namecheap – Domain name registrar

- CheapAir.com – Travel booking site for airline tickets, car rentals, hotels
- Expedia.com – Online travel booking agency
- Gift – Buy gift cards using Bitcoin
- Newegg.com – Online electronics retailer now uses bitpay to accept Bitcoin as payment
- Wikipedia – The Free Encyclopedia with 4 570 000+ articles
- Steam – Desktop gaming platform
- Alza – Largest Czech online retailer
- The Internet Archive – web documentation company
- Bitcoin.Travel – a travel site that provides accommodation, apartments, attractions, bars, and beauty salons around the world
- Pembury Tavern – A pub in London, England
- Old Fitzroy – A pub in Sydney, Australia
- The Pink Cow – A diner in Tokyo, Japan
- The Pirate Bay – BitTorrent directories
- Zynga – Mobile gaming
- 4Chan.org – For premium services
- EZTV – Torrents TV shows provider
- Mega.co.nz – The new venture started by the former owner of MegaUpload Kim Dotcom

- Lumfile – Free cloud base file server – pay for premium services
- Etsy Vendors – 93 of them
- PizzaForCoins.com – Domino's Pizza signed up – pay for their pizza with Bitcoins
- Whole Foods – Organic food store (by purchasing gift card from Gyft)
- Bitcoincoffee.com – Buy your favorite coffee online
- Grass Hill Alpacas – A local farm in Haydenville, MA
- Jeffersons Store – A street wear clothing store in Bergenfield, N.J
- Helen's Pizza – Jersey City, N.J., you can get a slice of pizza for 0.00339 Bitcoin by pointing your phone at a sign next to the cash register
- A Class Limousine – Pick you up and drop you off at Newark (N.J.) Airport
- Seoclerks.com – Get SEO work done on your site cheap
- Mint.com – Mint pulls all your financial accounts into one place. Set a budget, track your goals and do more
- Fancy.com – Discover amazing stuff, collect the things you love, buy it all in one place (Source: Fancy)

- Bloomberg.com – Online newspaper
- Humblebundle.com – Indie game site
- BigFishGames.com – Games for PC, Mac and Smartphones (iPhone, Android, Windows)
- Suntimes.com – Chicago based online newspaper
- San Jose Earthquakes – San Jose California Professional Soccer Team (MLS)
- Crowdtilt.com – The fastest and easiest way to pool funds with family and friends (Source: crowdtilt)
- Lumfile – Server Company that offers free cloud-based servers
- Museum of the Coastal Bend – 2200 East Red River Street, Victoria, Texas 77901, USA
- Gap, GameStop and JC Penney – have to use eGifter.com
- Etsy Vendors – Original art and Jewelry creations
- Fight for the Future – Leading organization finding for Internet freedom
- i-Pmart (ipmart.com.my) – A Malaysian online mobile phone and electronic parts retailer
- curryupnow.com – A total of 12 restaurants on the list of restaurants accept Bitcoins in San Francisco Bay Area

- Dish Network – An American direct-broadcast satellite service provider
- The Libertarian Party – United States political party
- Yacht-base.com – Croatian yacht charter company
- Euro Pacific – A major precious metal dealer
- CEX – The trade-in chain has a shop in Glasgow, Scotland that accepts Bitcoin
- Straub Auto Repairs – 477 Warburton Ave, Hastings-on-Hudson, NY 10706 – (914) 478-1177
- PSP Mollie – Dutch Payment Service
- Intuit – an American software company that develops financial and tax preparation software and related services for small businesses, accountants and individuals.
- ShopJoy – An Australian online retailer that sells novelty and unique gifts
- Lv.net – Las Vegas high-speed internet services
- ExpressVPN.com – High speed, ultra secure VPN network
- Grooveshark – Online music streaming service based in the United States
- Braintree – Well known payments processor
- MIT Coop Store – Massachusetts Institute of Technology student bookstore

- SimplePay – Nigeria's most popular web and mobile-based wallet service
- SFU bookstore – Simon Fraser University in Vancouver, Canada
- State Republican Party – First State Republican Party to accept Bitcoin donations (http://www.lagop.com/bitcoin-donate)
- mspinc.com – Respiratory medical equipment supplies store
- Shopify.com – An online store that allows anyone to sell their products
- Famsa – Mexico's biggest retailer
- Naughty America – Adult entertainment provider
- Mexico's Universidad de las Américas Puebla – A major university in Mexico
- LOT Polish Airlines – A worldwide airline based in Poland
- MovieTickets.com – Online movie ticket exchange/retailer
- Dream Lover – Online relationship service
- Lionsgate Films – The production studio behind titles such as The Hunger Games and The Day After Tomorrow
- Rakutan – A Japanese e-commerce giant
- Badoo – Online dating network

- RE/MAX London – UK-based franchisee of the global real estate network
- T-Mobile Poland – T-Mobile's Poland-based mobile phone top-up company
- Stripe – san Francisco-based Payments Company
- WebJet – Online travel agency
- Green Man Gaming – Popular digital game reseller
- Save the Children – Global charity organization
- NCR Silver – Point of sales systems
- One Shot Hotels – Spanish hotel chain
- Coupa Café in Palo Alto
- PureVPN – VPN provider
- That's my face – create action figures
- Foodler – North American restaurant delivery company
- Amagi Metals – Precious metal furnisher
- Amazon – An online company that sells almost anything.

Among others.

CHAPTER 8

WHERE DO YOU STORE BITCOIN?

Here are a few ways to store your Bitcoins that may be safer than others.

1.   Online Bitcoin wallets

Wallets that can be accessed on the web from any internet connected device.

2.   Desktop Wallet

A desktop wallet offers a number of advantages over an online wallet. While online wallets are easily accessed from anywhere in the world, they are also more vulnerable to potential hacking. Desktop wallets, on the other hand, are accessed only via your private computer, with personal security keys stored just on that machine. Thus, exposure of your security key online is reduced. Nonetheless, desktop wallets are still susceptible to hacks if your machine is infected with malware designed to root out keys and steal Bitcoins.

3.   Hardware Wallet

More secure than a desktop wallet is a hardware wallet. These wallets are bits of hardware, external devices like USB drives which you can carry around on your person. An added benefit of a hardware wallet is the complete anonymity with which you can transact. There is no personal information linked to the hardware, so no identifying data which could be leaked. Hardware wallets are resilient to malware, and if you happen to lose the wallet you'll be able to recover the funds using a seed phrase.

4.   Paper Wallet

A paper wallet is also a relatively safe way of storing Bitcoin, although it requires a bit more advanced understanding of how digital currencies work. Generate a paper wallet online using any number of dedicated websites, or generate the wallet offline for even greater security. Paper wallets are stored easily because they don't take up a great deal of space, and they also offer true anonymity: they are simply a Bitcoin seed written in some way on a piece of paper.

CHAPTER 9

THE KEY FOUNDERS OF BITCOIN AND DIGITAL CURRENCY

Satoshi Nakamoto is the name used by the unknown person(s) who designed Bitcoin and created its original reference implementation. As part of the implementation, they also devised the first blockchain database. In the process, they were the first to solve the double spending problem for the digital currency. They were active in the development of Bitcoin up until December 2010.

Nakamoto claimed to be a man living in Japan, born on 5 April 1975. However, speculation about the true identity of Nakamoto has mostly focused on a number of cryptography and computer science experts of non-Japanese descent, living in the United States and Europe.

As of 24 May 2017, Nakamoto is believed to own up to roughly one million Bitcoins, with a value estimated at approximately $4.7 billion USD as of August 2017.

In October 2008, Nakamoto published a paper on The Cryptography Mailing list at metzdowd.com describing the Bitcoin digital currency. It was titled Bitcoin: A Peer-to-Peer Electronic Cash System. In January 2009, Nakamoto released the first Bitcoin software that launched the network and the first units of the Bitcoin cryptocurrency, called Bitcoins. Satoshi Nakamoto released the Version 0.1 of Bitcoin software on Source forge on 9 January 2009.

Nakamoto claimed that work on the writing of the code began in 2007. The inventor of Bitcoin knew that due to its nature, the core design would have to be able to support a broad range of transaction types. The implemented solution enabled specialized codes and data fields from the start through the use of a predictive script.

Nakamoto created a website with the domain name bitcoin.org and continued to collaborate with other developers on the Bitcoin software until mid-2010.

Around this time, he handed over control of the source code repository and network alert key to Gavin Andresen, transferred several related domains to various prominent members of the Bitcoin community, and stopped his involvement in the project. Until shortly before his absence and handover, Nakamoto made all modifications to the source code himself.

HOW BITCOIN KEEPS YOUR IDENTITY A SECRET

Bitcoin is anonymous, but not private: identities are nowhere recorded in the Bitcoin protocol itself, but every transaction performed with Bitcoin is visible on the distributed electronic public ledger known as the blockchain.

The anonymity provided by Bitcoin is at once a point of attraction and a challenge for financial regulation. As the pace of adoption of the currency grows and as it comes under scrutiny by the legal and financial systems, particularly with regard to compliance with applicable anti-money laundering (AML) statutes and know-your-customer (KYC) controls, its true level of anonymity will become an increasingly closely studied subject.

For many users of Bitcoin, who access the currency through one of the popular online wallet or exchange services, their participation at the outset entails linking their personal identity to their Bitcoin holdings. Bitcoin for these users is effectively no more anonymous than a bank account, although this loss of anonymity takes place at the point of entry into the currency and is not a feature of the Bitcoin protocol itself.

For those who wish to take advantage of Bitcoin's intrinsic anonymity, they must find an alternative entry point, such as acquiring Bitcoin in a private transaction, as compensation for goods or services rendered, or as a reward for mining. Subsequent Bitcoin transactions can then be anonymous since real-world identities are not recorded on the blockchain ledger: the only identifying information recorded there are the Bitcoin addresses, whose corresponding private keys are held by the owners as proof of ownership.

CHAPTER 10

THE BEST PLATFORMS USED TO TRADE BITCOIN

Based on research, here are the best platforms used to trade Bitcoin.

- Coinbase
- Plus500
- AvaTrade
- eToro
- IG
- XTB
- Markets.com
- Trade.com
- Admiral Markets
- UFX
- Ayrex

Among others.

HOW IS BITCOIN DIFFERENT THAN PAPER CURRENCY?

Bitcoin is a virtual currency. It doesn't exist in the kind of physical form that the currency & coin we're used to exist in. It doesn't even exist in a form as physical as Monopoly money. It is electrons – not molecules. But consider how much cash you personally handle. You get a paycheck that you take to the bank – or its auto deposited without you even seeing the paper that it's not printed on. You then use a debit card (or a checkbook) to access those funds. At best, you see 10% of it in a cash form in your pocket or in your pocketbook. So, it turns out that 90% of the funds that you manage are virtual – electrons in a spreadsheet or database.

1.   Volatility

It may seem, that Bitcoin is too volatile and the price jumps like crazy.

Compared to USD, EUR, GBP - Yes; Compared to the currency of Ukraine, Argentina and dozens of other currencies it's much more stable.

2.   Value

Bitcoin is deflationary

This means that supply is limited and no one can just print more of it.

In the USSR there was a day when the government decided to divide the value of its official currency by 10. With Bitcoin, that is not possible.

3.   Transaction fees

Western Union or other similar services usually take 1–5% for a transfer of money. With Bitcoin, the usual transaction fee is a couple of cents and you can even pay less if you're not in a hurry.

4.   Portability

As long as you are able to store 256 bits you can have Bitcoins (99% of computers can do this). You can write the key at the piece of paper or even remember it.

5.   Transferability

The usual transaction time is negligible (<1s). But if your transaction is extremely important you need to wait for 6 blocks (6 confirmations) which is usually around 1 hour.

6.   Security

If your bank goes down - there is no recourse, except for FDIC insurance. With Bitcoin, not much can go wrong unless you lose the key.

7.   Deniability

The bank is a single point of failure. If your bank goes down – it goes down hard. Bitcoin has a distributed nature, which makes it extremely resilient to different types of attacks. A hacker or team of hackers will need to simultaneously infect millions of computers or points of access successfully at the same time.

8.   Divisibility:

You can have/buy/transfer as little as ~0.0000071411 USD (at current price) in Bitcoin. It's the smallest unit and it equals to 0.00000001 BTC.

CHAPTER 11

FUN FACTS ABOUT BITCOIN

The most popular type of virtual currency is known as Bitcoin and has steadily begun to rise in popularity and strength over the years. At first glance, Bitcoin may sound confusing, however, below are a few Bitcoin fun facts to ease your mind.

1.   No one single entity controls this currency

Bitcoin is open-source software, which means anyone and everyone can access it. The same way you connect to a website and download some images or songs, the same way you can get Bitcoin. Also, no company stands behind the creation of Bitcoin, thus, since the creator is anonymous, there is no owner.

2.   There is a finite number of Bitcoins

As mentioned previously, there is a limited number of Bitcoins, and that's one of the main reasons why it's stable and why it has a certain value. Everything that is limited on this earth has fantastic value, and just as other materials or substances have incredible value because of their rarity and limited quantity, Bitcoins have the same quality.

3.   Bitcoins have no inherent or set value

This is another fact why Bitcoin has unique and stable value. There is no other currency or anything from which Bitcoin inherited its worth. Bitcoin has a certain value, but it varies depending on what services were provided for them.

4.   You can see all the transactions

Since it is software that is available for anyone, everything regarding Bitcoins including detailed reports of the operations is also available. There is no one person behind this currency, meaning the information is not controlled by anyone. You can easily search on the Internet for all the detailed information about the Bitcoin transactions and be sure that you will find what you're looking for.

5.   You can mine Bitcoins

As it was already stated earlier, there are many ways for you to get Bitcoin and one of the most efficient of these is called "mining." This term is used for those who earn Bitcoins by solving math problems while using special software that will distribute a certain amount of Bitcoins in exchange for those solutions. The people that do this kind of work are so-called "miners." This is one of the most interesting ways of implementing a currency as well as it motivates people to deal with mathematical problems.

6.	You cannot reverse a transaction to be forced to pay

Once a transaction using Bitcoin is made, there is no going back. In other words, a transaction cannot be reversed. You can trust the security of operations because you will be forced to use a website that handles them correctly. Also, you don't need to be concerned about being forced to pay for something just because this is a digital currency, it's the same as regular money... If you don't want to pay for something, you don't have to.

7.	You can send money with little to no fees

When you use Bitcoins, there are no fees when it comes to sending money to someone, because there is no one that owns Bitcoin, thus there is no one to make a profit out of those transfers.

8.   Bitcoins are held in digital wallets

If you were wondering where you will keep your Bitcoins, it's simple; you will have a wallet of course, but a digital one. It's the same thing as with bank account only it has a different name, and you don't have to pay any annual or monthly fees to keep that wallet. It acts as a physical wallet, and you will have your Bitcoins in one place from where you can do whatever you want with them.

9.   Losing your wallet means those Bitcoins are lost forever

The most dangerous part of the Bitcoins is that you cannot get them back unless the other side repays you the sum. This is why you must take care of the security of your Bitcoin wallet as well as operate only with trusted vendors. Losing your wallet will put you in a position where you cannot get them back in any way, so be careful when storing and spending them.

10.   You can buy items or services with Bitcoins

You will be able to purchase anything as long as the provider of those goods accepts the payment in Bitcoins. This is becoming more and more popular, and you will find more things at your disposal which you can pay for with Bitcoin. As stated above, there are more than 100 companies accepting Bitcoin worldwide.

11.   You can have anonymity

This is one of the best perks of Bitcoin; there is no trace back to you, and that is the main reason why more countries are banning and prohibiting the use of this currency. You can pay for anything with Bitcoin and remain completely anonymous.

12.   Limited supply

You must be aware of this at all time, there is a small number of Bitcoins that are available online, and that's it. This is the main reason for the stability of this currency as well as its value. Spend you Bitcoins carefully, and there will always be the same amount of Bitcoins in circulation.

13.   Companies and websites are now accepting Bitcoin

This is a great way for you to buy what you need because there are still many merchants that support Bitcoin and accept payments via Bitcoin currency.

14.   Death of MT GOX

Mt Gox was a company that was handling almost 70% of all the transactions based on Bitcoin, and at the time of the crash, it was holding over 850,000 Bitcoins, which was valued to be the same as $450 million dollars at the time. Now, 850,000 bitcoins is worth roughly $4 billion at the time of writing this book.

That accident is considered to be one of the biggest thieveries of all time, and since the Bitcoin is virtually untraceable, they only managed to retrieve 200,000 Bitcoins. However, preventative measures have been put in place within exchanges to prevent something like this from ever happening again.

15. The end of mining

The end of the "mining" is inevitable since there is only a limited number of Bitcoins which will be introduced into the market. Therefore, the actual end of "mining" will be when the last Bitcoin is mined. When there are no Bitcoins left, there will be no need for miners. Some estimates put this year at 2050, while others stretch it out past year 2140.

16. Frequent shift in value

This is something that is also inevitable when it comes to the stability of the currency. The more Bitcoins there are, the lower the value will be, the fewer Bitcoins there are, and the better the value will be. This is a fact, and is something that needs to be taken into consideration when investing in Bitcoin.

17.   Government seizure

The main reason for banning this currency is because of illegal and sometimes terrorist activity being funded. This "anonymity" is a problem because you can easily purchase anything illegal and no one can know who bought it. They can't trace the Bitcoin back to you. On the other hand, illegal activity and terrorist funding happens in all forms of currency, so it's more of the pot calling the kettle black.

18.   American regulation

There are many questions when it comes to Bitcoin and its legality, but frankly, the situation is that the validity status varies from country to country. There are those countries that support Bitcoin, and there are those that don't. You will have to check online which country supports it and which doesn't, but that information is easily acquired. The USA is also looking to control and regulate Bitcoin altogether, which is not something that anyone wants.

18. Physical Bitcoin

The same way there is a digital Bitcoin, there is also a physical Bitcoin, which is pretty much the same thing as the digital, and it also holds a piece of digital information. There are fewer companies and markets that deal with physical Bitcoins than the ones that are working with digital Bitcoins.

19. Pizza was the first thing purchased using Bitcoin

After the first Bitcoin transaction took place between Satoshi and Hal Finney in 2009, the first recorded purchase was made for buying pizza worth $25. To do so, 10,000 Bitcoins were spent.

20. The Bitcoin network is much more powerful than supercomputers

According to experts, Bitcoin networks have a computing power of 2,046,364 Pflop/s. If you go ahead and combine the computing power of the 500 most powerful supercomputers, you'll get a combined fever of 274 Pflop/s.

21.   Bitcoin has been sent into outer space

In 2016, Genesis Mining, a Bitcoin cloud mining provider, set Bitcoin to space. This was done using a 3D Bitcoin model and a Bitcoin paper wallet, which was tied to a weather balloon. The whole journey was recorded using a GoPro focused on the model and wallet. Once the weather balloon reached a height of 20 kilometers, the ground team made the transaction to the paper wallet. Another transfer was made to the wallet once it achieved the maximum possible altitude of 34 km.

22.   Bitcoin is highly volatile

Since its launch in the past decade Bitcoin has become one of the most important phenomena in the digital world. Its price has touched thousands of dollars. However, the price keeps fluctuating and it remains volatile. Predictions have also been made that Bitcoin might fall in the future if it follows the current path. This is because of a small number of people, about 10, control the majority of Bitcoin. This defeats the entire decentralized nature of currency. On the other hand, some say a single Bitcoin has the potential to reach hundreds of thousands and even millions of dollars each, come the end of mining.

23.   Black Friday Bitcoin sale

This is the place where you can get Bitcoin for cash, and then further use them to purchase anything there is available to be purchased using this currency. The best way for you to get Bitcoins is on Black Friday.

24.   Governments will try to control Bitcoin and will most likely fail

As Bitcoin becomes more pervasive, experts predict governments will try to control it, try to understand more detail about how it is being used and try to monitor its use in the digital economy. However, because of the structure of Bitcoin, and the encryption and anonymity which is baked into the blockchain, there is very little opportunity to control this. The only clear way for nation states to control the distribution of the currency would be for them to buy up the supply and stockpile Bitcoin, as many have done with gold.

Regardless of what Bitcoin is being used for, the key takeaway is that it is being used more and more widely and that this expanding use is resulting in a corresponding uplift in value which shows no sign of slowing anytime soon.

PREDICTIONS AS TO WHAT THE PRICE OF BITCOIN MAY BECOME IN THE FUTURE

All over the internet you can find forecasts and predictions by analysts, Bitcoin followers or enthusiasts pulling out facts to support their imagination of where will the prices reach. Sometimes impossible or too good to be true.

From Max Keiser who pointed out his view of BTC rising above $10,000 to analyst and expert Ronnie Moas that stated Bitcoin against the US Dollar could reach $15k – $20k in late 2020.

At the start of August 2017, SegWit protocol locked-in and activated while followed by the Lightning Network concept being tested out which was made possible of the Segregated Witness malleability fix – BTC market cap moved and positioned itself very close to the $80 billion market capitalization which represents 50% domination of the total virtual currency market cap. That would be 1% of golds and just $50 million away from the MasterCard market cap. Others estimate a $5 trillion market cap.

Within the next 2-3 years, the mining and Bitcoin creation will drop by half leaving only around 850 that will be formed/day. Continuing 4 years later – 2024 only 430 will be created and so on.

Approx just over the 2030 mark (2032) close to 99 percent of all Bitcoin that will exist will be already created and mined on the network. The next 1.6% will be a war to get their hands on them.

With the mainstream factor taking global scale everyday and more, at one point the fear of being left out will make people panic as they understand there is not much Bitcoin to be circulated around. Proportionally with the demand at that point, the price will play its role and rise. If the same event takes place this year (in 2017) like it did last summer, Bitcoin could easily be reaching over the $20,000 mark in late or approx 2020.

COULD BITCOIN RISE TO $1 MILLION?

Theoretically, yes, although consider what that would mean. A price of $1 million each would translate to a total value of $16.35 trillion for all of the Bitcoins in existence. Currently, the total value of Bitcoin is about $39 billion.

Meanwhile, the U.S. money supply (M2), which includes all physical currency, demand deposits, savings accounts, and money market accounts, is about $13.5 trillion. And this is just one country's money supply -- Bitcoin, on the other hand, is a truly international currency. In fact, U.S.-based transactions are one of the smaller sources of Bitcoin volume. With that in mind, consider that the global M2 money supply is estimated to be about $68.7 trillion, expressed in U.S. dollars.

Experts point out that while Bitcoin would have to work a little to become a major player in the global currency market, the total Bitcoin market value at $1 million each isn't an outlandish amount of money.

E.g.: If the price of Bitcoin is $2,400 to $1 million, it would represent a rather mild gain when compared to the gains of the past seven years. In fact, $100 worth of Bitcoin purchased seven years ago, when a Bitcoin was worth approximately $0.003, would be worth roughly $80 million today, a gain of about 800,000%. Meanwhile, a jump from $2,400 to $1 million would represent a gain of "only" 42,000%.

Some analysts fear that if Bitcoin did actually propose this kind of threat on a global scale, nations would begin banning the use of and transactions involving Bitcoin, as to avoid devaluing their own currency form people no longer using it. This, however, remains to be seen.

CONCLUSION

Bitcoin (BTC) is a relatively new kind of digital currency - with cryptographic keys - that is decentralized to a network of computers used by users and miners around the world and is not controlled by a single organization or government. While the technology is new, the idea is a smidge older. It is the first digital cryptocurrency that has gained the public's attention and is accepted by a growing number of merchants. Like other currencies, users can use the digital currency to buy goods and services online as well as in some physical stores that accept it as a form of payment. Currency traders can also trade Bitcoins in Bitcoin exchanges.

In conclusion,

1.   Bitcoin does not have a centralized authority or clearing house (e.g. government, central bank, MasterCard or Visa network). The peer-to-peer payment network is managed by users and miners around the world. The currency is anonymously transferred directly between users through the internet without going through a clearing house.

This means that transaction fees are much lower and processing times are much quicker.

2. Bitcoin is created through a process called "Bitcoin mining". Miners around the world use mining software and computers to solve complex Bitcoin algorithms to approve Bitcoin transactions. They are awarded transaction fees and new Bitcoins generated from solving Bitcoin algorithms.

3. There is a limited number of Bitcoins in circulation. The difficulty to mine Bitcoins (solve algorithms) becomes harder as more Bitcoins are generated, and the maximum amount in circulation is capped at 21 million. The limit will not be reached until approximately the year 2140, with an overwhelming majority having been mined by 2050. This makes Bitcoins more valuable as more people use them.

4. A public ledger called 'Blockchain' records all Bitcoin transactions and shows each Bitcoin owner's respective holdings. Anyone can access the public ledger to verify transactions. This makes the digital currency more transparent and predictable. More

importantly, the transparency prevents fraud and double spending of the same Bitcoins.

5.   The digital currency can be acquired through Bitcoin mining or Bitcoin exchanges.

6.   Bitcoin wallets (similar to PayPal accounts) are used for storing Bitcoins, private keys, and public addresses as well as for anonymously transferring Bitcoins between users.

Bitcoins are not insured and are not protected by government agencies. Hence, they cannot be recovered if the secret keys are stolen or lost to a failed hard drive, or due to the closure of a Bitcoin exchange. If the secret keys are lost, the associated Bitcoins cannot be recovered and would then be out of circulation. An event like this would be tragic for some, and extremely beneficial for others who held onto their Bitcoins. Supply and demand is Bitcoins best friend.

Made in the USA
Columbia, SC
21 October 2018